Super Gay

Written by Jessi Hersey
Illustrations by: Ray B
Edited by: Taylor Fay

Dedicated to anyone with a pronoun and everyone that can relate. To any child that hold this book to read it. A special thank you to Ed for calling my outfit for Gay Pride Super Gay it helped inspire this story. Thank you also to Molly C (MC) for reminding me the importance of pronouns, which was a huge inspiration behind this idea. Thank you to all my friends and family that are in constant support of all my endeavors. I appreciate you all. And most importantly, thank you, God, for always being here.

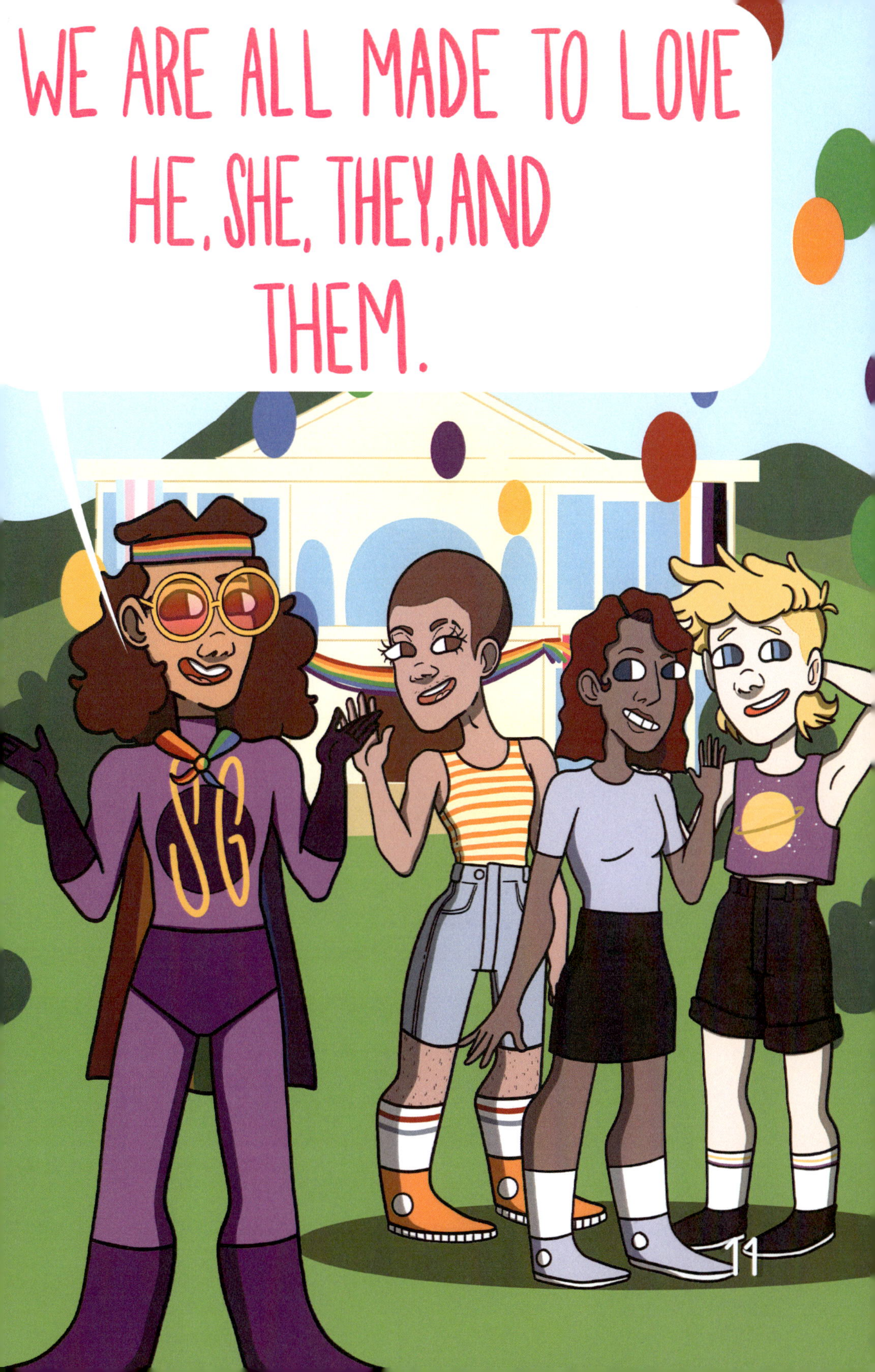
WE ARE ALL MADE TO LOVE HE, SHE, THEY, AND THEM.
SG

SO, LET'S CELEBRATE LOVE
IN THE BEST WAY
WE CAN!

www.ingramcontent.com/pod-product-compliance
Lightning Source LLC
Chambersburg PA
CBRC090825120626
46547CB00007B/608